# CASA LOMA

## CANADA'S FAIRY-TALE CASTLE AND ITS OWNER, SIR HENRY PELLATT

BILL FREEMAN

PHOTOGRAPHY BY VINCENZO PIETROPAOLO

JAMES LORIMER AND COMPANY, PUBLISHERS
TORONTO, 1998

James Lorimer & Company acknowledges the support of the Department of Canadian Heritage and the Ontario Arts Council in the development of writing and publishing in Canada. We acknowledge the support of the Canada Council for the Arts for our publishing program.

Cover photo by Vincenzo Pietropaolo

**Canadian Cataloguing in Publication Data**

Freeman, Bill, 1938-
    Casa Loma: Toronto's fairy-tale castle and its owner,
    Sir Henry Pellatt
ISBN 1-55028-595-5
1. Casa Loma (Toronto, Ont.).  2. Pellatt, Henry Mill, Sir, 1859-1939. 3. Toronto (Ont.) - Buildings, structures, etc. I. Title.
FC3097.8.C37F73 1998     728.8'09713'541
C98-930210-5             F1059.5.T688C37 1998

James Lorimer & Company Ltd., Publishers
35 Britain Street
Toronto, Ontario
M5A 1R7

Printed and bound in Canada

## Photo Credits

Except for the following images, all photographs in this book were taken by Vincenzo Pietropaolo.

Casa Loma: 9 (top), 11, 12, 14 (top), 15 (left), 31, 34 (bottom), 42, 47 (top), 48 (top), 55, 56, 65 (bottom)

City of Toronto Archives: 8 (right), 34 (top), 35, 39 (top), 40 (top and bottom right), 41, 43, 44 (bottom), 45, 47, 49, 50, 52, 53, 54, 57 (bottom), 58, 59, 60, 61, 62, 65 (top), 67, 68

Metro Reference Library: 46

Ontario Hydro Archives: 43 (top), 44 (top)

Queen's Own Rifles: 36, 37 (top), 48 (bottom), 51, 69, 70

Albert Fulton: 66

We thank these organizations and individuals for their assistance and, in some cases, permission to reproduce these images.

Every effort has been made to trace the ownership of all copyrighted material reproduced in this book. We regret any errors and will be pleased to make any necessary corrections in future editions.

# Contents

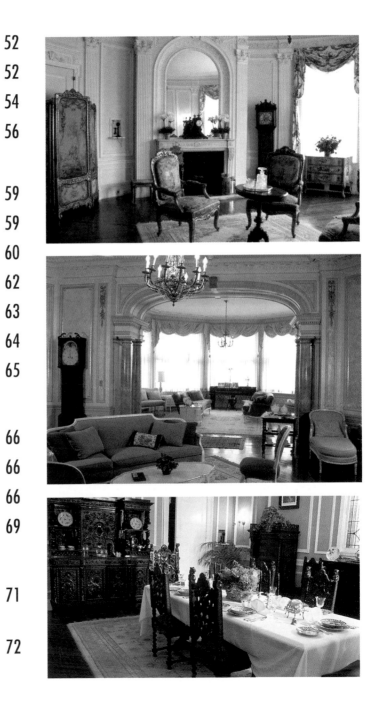

# ACKNOWLEDGMENTS

A book such as this is more a collective effort than the product of any one person and I am indebted to many people who generously shared their research and information about Casa Loma and the Pellatt family.

Vince Pietropaolo's spectacular photos capture the spirit of the castle. He spent many hours searching for details and waiting for the right light. His efforts are here for all to enjoy.

I would also like to thank Virginia Cooper, Chief Executive Officer of Casa Loma, and her staff. Without their help and cooperation it would not have been possible to do this book. Joan Crosbie, the curator of Casa Loma, devoted hours to this project. Her knowledge of the various artifacts in the castle and the many files that she made available were particularly useful.

Peter Simundson, the archivist of the Queen's Own Rifles Regiment, went out of his way to help. He provided many of the historical photos of the regiment in these pages as well as useful background information.

When I happened to mention to my friend Albert Fulton, archivist and historian par excellence, that I was working on this project, he arrived at my door with a big file containing a sheaf of photos and other collectibles about Casa Loma. I found all of it helpful and some of that material appears in these pages. Albert also suggested where I might find some newspaper articles that I would have otherwise missed.

I would also like to thank the staff of James Lorimer & Company Ltd., Publishers. Diane Young offered helpful editorial advice. Jim Lorimer was never far from this project. He read the manuscript at different stages and made a number of useful suggestions. Jennifer Gillard collected pictures and made sure that everything was assembled. The staff at Formac, in Halifax, had to put up with constantly expanding text and pictures. Thanks to their efforts all the different elements of this project were pulled together.

— B. F.

# FLOOR PLANS

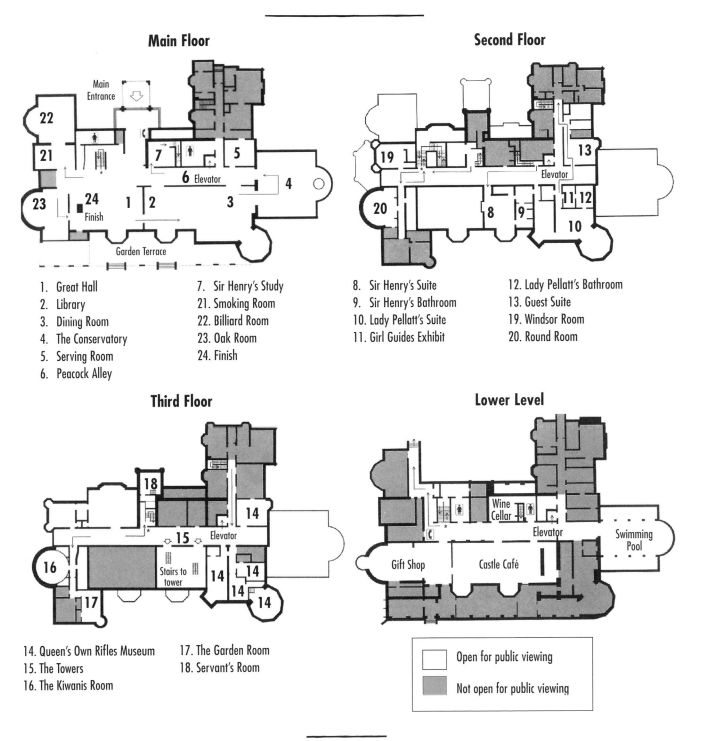

## Main Floor

Main Entrance

22 21 23 24 Finish 1 2 7 6 Elevator 5 3 4

Garden Terrace

1. Great Hall
2. Library
3. Dining Room
4. The Conservatory
5. Serving Room
6. Peacock Alley

7. Sir Henry's Study
21. Smoking Room
22. Billiard Room
23. Oak Room
24. Finish

## Second Floor

19 20 8 9 Elevator 13 11 12 10

8. Sir Henry's Suite
9. Sir Henry's Bathroom
10. Lady Pellatt's Suite
11. Girl Guides Exhibit

12. Lady Pellatt's Bathroom
13. Guest Suite
19. Windsor Room
20. Round Room

## Third Floor

18 15 16 17 14 Elevator 14 14 14 14

Stairs to tower

14. Queen's Own Rifles Museum
15. The Towers
16. The Kiwanis Room

17. The Garden Room
18. Servant's Room

## Lower Level

Wine Cellar

Gift Shop    Castle Café    Elevator    Swimming Pool

|  | Open for public viewing |
|---|---|
|  | Not open for public viewing |

## Chapter 1

# WALKING TOUR

Casa Loma, with its towers and turrets, gargoyles and heraldic figures, elegant grey stone walls and red tile roof, is one of the most striking, if not the most eccentric, homes in Canada. "The Castle," as it is known, remains a fascinating place—a reminder of our link to the British Empire and an expression of the flamboyant business style in the early part of the twentieth century.

Built by Sir Henry Pellatt between 1911 and 1914, and designed by E.J. Lennox, one of the leading architects of the day, Casa Loma was intended to be a grand home in the tradition of English manor-houses and the great mansions constructed by the wealthy in the United States at that time. It achieved this goal in flamboyant style, but it also became an expression of Sir Henry's fascinating life and obsessions.

*Heraldic figure, Casa Loma roof.*

In the decades prior to World War I, Canadians were just beginning to realize the potential of their country. Railways were completed through to the Pacific coast, the agricultural lands of the Prairie Provinces were rapidly settled, mines in Northern Ontario and the west were opened, trade expanded, and Toronto emerged as an important financial, manufacturing, and administrative centre of the new nation.

Sir Henry was perfectly suited to these times and the young country. He was a big, expansive man, optimistic, confident of his own abilities, innovative, daring in his business dealings and generous as a benefactor. Pellatt had a lifelong involvement with the Canadian militia. He was a strong supporter of British royalty and loved the pageantry and ceremony that came with those interests. Many found him pompous and dull, but many more admired his accomplishments and marvelled at the way he spread his money around to rich and poor alike.

Like Pellatt himself, Casa Loma has a style that is larger than life. It was the biggest private home ever built in Canada, with ninety-eight rooms. The building took three hundred men three years to complete. Its cost of $3.5 million (more than $100 million in today's values) was a staggering amount of money. The original furnishings alone cost $1.5 million.

In every way Casa Loma was designed to impress and overwhelm. Large rooms panelled in the most expensive, hand-carved woods; fireplace mantels worth a small fortune; floors laid in intricate designs; two massive towers that soared above the tallest trees; and the greatest private art collection in Canada at the time. And yet the story of Casa Loma ended in spectacular failure. The castle came to be called "Pellatt's Folly" by many because it played a significant role in the financial collapse of one of Canada's greatest fortunes.

And yet time has proven that Casa Loma is anything but a failure. Today visitors from around the world marvel at the sheer size of the building and its many features. Sir Henry lost his castle, but in the process we have gained an unparalleled landmark to explore and enjoy.

*Sir Henry, 1911.*

# THE CASTLE EXTERIOR

The castles of Europe were the source of inspiration for Casa Loma. In medieval times there was a compelling need for the impregnable fortress, designed to repel enemies, but Toronto in the early part of the twentieth century was hardly in danger of attack from barbaric hordes. Casa Loma was not built for defence, but rather to create an impression of grandeur.

Sir Henry Pellatt was a financier of considerable affluence, and he wanted

*Northern view of Casa Loma.*

to impress his various associates with his wealth and power. He also commanded the largest militia unit in Canada and had a great fascination with all things military. He decided that he wanted to build a great home where he could live in regal style, so it is not surprising that the result was a fantasy castle with battlements, towers, and vast rooms filled with every available amenity.

Perched on the brow of a hill overlooking the city, six hundred feet above the level of Lake Ontario, which can be seen in the distance, Casa Loma is located on one of the most impressive pieces of property in Toronto.

The castle is immense. The height from the ground to the top of the Scottish tower is more than 130 feet. Foundations at some points go forty-five feet underground. Casa Loma is characterized by a complicated skyline of white cast-stone battlements, chimneys, and towers. Such care was taken to maintain the medieval impression that down-spouts were buried so as not to detract from the illusion. The solid stone wall that surrounds the castle is six feet wide, ten feet high, and four or more feet deep. Every effort was made to make the building and the property appear vast, impressive, and impregnable.

# THE GREAT HALL

Just as the outside of Casa Loma was designed to impress anyone who might pass by, the interior was to be awe inspiring. When visitors called, they would first be ushered into the great hall. In size and dimensions this is the most imposing room in the castle. Its ceiling is sixty feet high and features a hammer-beam roof.

*Sir Henry's portrait, about 1900.*

floor. Cheerful gargoyles grace the supporting columns. On the south wall is a grand, forty-foot-high leaded glass window with 738 individual panes of glass.

One item of particular interest is the coronation chair. This is an exact replica of the chair that sits in Westminster Abbey in London, England, and

Along the north wall is a bridge walkway where people can look over the rail into the hall from the second

has been used in the coronation of every British monarch for the last seven hundred years.

*The fireplace at the eastern end of the Great Hall.*

*The Wurlitzer organ in front of a soaring forty-foot window.*

# THE LIBRARY

*The Library is used today for banquets.*

a floor strong enough to hold the heaviest military equipment.

The library has space for ten thousand books. The Pellatts were not known for their passion for literature, but they filled the shelves with books on imperial and military history and gardening. The ceiling is plastered in Elizabethan style with the Pellatt family crest and motto, *Devant si je puis* (Foremost if I can), moulded into the plaster. Sir Henry lived by that motto in all aspects of his life.

The library, just to the east of the great hall, was a room especially enjoyed by Sir Henry and Lady Mary Pellatt. The herring-bone hardwood floor creates an interesting visual illusion. When you look across the floor you can see stripes of light and dark wood, but when you look at the floor beneath your feet, the wood is one colour.

Sir Henry took a special interest when the floor was laid. He inspected it every day. If there were any squeaks, he would insist that it be torn up and relaid. The wooden floor lies on an eighteen-inch-thick base of concrete, strong enough to bear the weight of a train locomotive. Sir Henry planned to turn Casa Loma into a military museum, and he wanted

*A detail of the Library bookshelves.*

# THE DINING ROOM

The Dining Room corner nook.

The wall between the library and the dining room has been taken down, but the pillars mark where the wall originally existed. The Pellatts loved to entertain. Regimental mess dinners for one hundred or more officers were frequently held here, and often Sir Henry would entertain his business associates.

The small corner nook was used by the Pellatts for more intimate dinner parties. The table and chairs in this room were part of the original furnishings of the castle. They were a gift from the estate of the Pellatts' only child, Reginald.

Rare oak clock, nineteenth century.

This glass cabinet displays some of the Pellatts' original china.

# THE CONSERVATORY

*The Conservatory, showing the stained-glass dome.*

The Pellatts were particularly fond of the conservatory, and often Lady Mary held tea parties and receptions in this room. Here exotic flowers and shrubs from around the world were displayed to their best advantage.

The marble floor in the conservatory was imported from Italy, while the marble facing on the flower beds came from a quarry in Bancroft. Steam pipes were buried in the flower beds to ensure the temperature of the soil was suitable all year long for the tropical plants.

The elaborate Italian stained-glass ceiling dome, which cost $12,000, was back-lit with six hundred light-

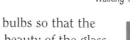

bulbs so that the beauty of the glass could be seen either by day or by night.

The bronze and glass doors leading into the conservatory are copies of a set made in New York for an Italian villa. Each of the doors cost $10,000.

*The bronze doors to the Conservatory. The figure on a pedestal is an elaborate barometer.*

# THE SERVING ROOM

*The Serving Room, showing the original furnishings.*

The serving room, just down the hall from the conservatory, was used as a smaller dining or breakfast room in the Pellatts' day. On bigger occasions staff used it as a serving area.

Most of the antiques in this room were part of the Casa Loma furniture purchased and used by the Pellatts. These elaborately carved pieces are typical of expensive household furnishings in the era prior to World War I.

Behind this room are the kitchens. The three original ovens were each big enough to roast a whole ox.

# PEACOCK ALLEY

Peacock Alley is an exact replica of a hallway of the same name at Windsor Castle in England.

The walls are virtually bare now, but once they were hung with the Pellatts' paintings and prints, said to be the greatest private collection of art in Canada at that time. Their pictures included Turners, Constables, a Rembrandt, and the paintings of many famous Canadian artists, such as Paul Peel and Cornelius Kreighoff. When Sir Henry lost his fortune, they were all sold in what was called "the auction of the century."

*Wood panelling in Peacock Alley.*

# SIR HENRY'S STUDY

*Sir Henry worked in this study.*

Sir Henry's study, just off Peacock Alley, is relatively small considering that he spent a great deal of time here working on his various business deals.

In Pellatt's day a copy of a desk used by Napoleon was in the centre of this room. Original art work hung on the walls above the Spanish mahogany panelling.

On one side of the fireplace is a secret passageway leading up to Sir Henry's bedroom suite, and on the other is a hidden stairway down to the wine cellar, where he kept one of the finest collections of wines in North America.

*There are secret passageways on either side of the Study fireplace.*

# SIR HENRY'S SUITE

*Sir Henry's Bedroom Suite is richly panelled in mahogany, but his furnishings were relatively simple.*

Both Sir Henry and Lady Mary had their own bedroom suites on the second floor of the castle. Lady Mary's suite, in fact, is considerably larger than Sir Henry's. This difference in the size of bedrooms was common among wealthy people at the time Casa Loma was built.

The original furnishings in Sir Henry's suite were quite plain but masculine. The room is panelled in mahogany with pilasters. Beside the marble fireplace is a hidden compartment

*A chest of drawers.*

where he kept important papers and valuables.

There were to be five thousand electric lights in Casa Loma, a remarkable number in that era. The system was designed so that Sir Henry could control all the lights from his bedroom; however, it never worked very well and was ultimately abandoned.

The only item of original furniture still in this room is the Phoenix lamp to the left of the bed.

# SIR HENRY'S BATH

*Sir Henry's shower.*

*The marble-lined bath.*

*The water heater for the shower.*

Sir Henry's white marble bathroom cost $10,000 when it was built. The shower has its own heater, and water sprayed out onto the bather from above and from the sides. Six large taps control the hot and cold water. All together Casa Loma has fifteen baths.

Sir Henry's bath even had a place for a telephone. There were fifty-nine telephones in the castle when the Pellatts lived there. The switchboard operator could handle more calls within Casa Loma than within the entire city of Toronto at that time.

# LADY MARY'S SUITE

*Lady Mary's bedroom, furnished in a style typical of the period.*

first electric elevator in a private home in the country. Despite this she spent a great deal of time in her bedroom suite and greatly enjoyed its sunny southern exposure.

The furnishings in these rooms are not the original ones, but they are in the style of the period. The Wedgwood blue and white on the walls were Lady Mary's favourite colours and were part of the original colour scheme.

The fireplace and mantel in this suite is one of twenty-two in Casa Loma. These were mainly decorative. The real heat for the castle came from a huge boiler that consumed eight hundred tons of coal a year.

Lady Mary's bedroom is a suite of rooms with a sitting room, bedroom, bathroom, and large balcony overlooking the city and the castle grounds. The sitting room is in the shape of a circle because it is within the base of the Scottish tower.

By the time the Pellatts moved into Casa Loma, Lady Mary was often confined to a wheelchair. Sir Henry installed an elevator in the building for her convenience, the

*The sitting room in Lady Mary's Suite.*

# THE GUEST SUITE

*The Guest Suite is a self-contained unit with its own bathroom and dressing room.*

The guest suite was the largest unit in the castle for visitors. Here friends of the couple and business or military associates of Sir Henry could live in relative privacy while staying at the grand house.

# THE SERVANT'S ROOM

*A servant's bedroom, furnished in a style typical of the period.*

It took a staff of forty to maintain Casa Loma. This was a great drain on Sir Henry, especially after he got into financial difficulties.

For long hours of work, servants could expect to be given their room and meals, as well as a modest salary. As this servant's room shows, their lodgings were Spartan.

Most of the Casa Loma servants were English and were recruited to come to Canada to work for the Pellatts. Until he got into difficulties, Sir Henry was known as a good, personable, and generous employer.

# THE WINDSOR ROOM

*The Windsor Room was reserved for royal guests.*

The Windsor room, named after the reigning British royal family, was set aside for royal guests.

The settee and chairs in the Windsor room are original. The fine detail in the ceiling and the fireplace mantel shows the quality of work that went into the building.

# THE ROUND ROOM

*The original furnishings in the Round Room illustrate the Pellatts' opulent style.*

The round room, built into the base of the west tower, is one of the most unique in the castle. All of the walls show the curvature of the tower, and even the windows and doors are shaped perfectly to fit the curve of the room.

The yellow colour on the walls, with the white highlights, gives a cheerful aspect to this room. The four elbow chairs and the three-fold screen were originally in the castle. They were purchased as part of the ongoing restoration program.

# THE SMOKING ROOM AND THE BILLIARD ROOM

*The fireplace is the focal point of the Smoking Room.*

The smoking room, on the ground floor in the northwest part of the castle, was designed as a place where the gentlemen retired after dinner to smoke their cigars, talk about the issues of the day, and tell stories.

*An elaborately carved cabinet in the Smoking Room (left) and panel detail (above).*

Just through the archway is the billiard room, where the men could play a friendly game on the full-sized Spanish mahogany table. Sir Henry and E.J. Lennox, the architect of Casa Loma, played a running game of billiards over the years, chalking up massive scores. They always left the scores standing for the next match so that neither of them was ever defeated.

*The magnificent Spanish mahogany billiard table, originally in this room, was sold by auction in 1924.*

# THE OAK ROOM

*The grandly furnished Oak Room was used for formal occasions.*

The oak room, or Napoleon drawing room as it was originally called, is the most elaborately decorated room in Casa Loma. This was the drawing room used for formal occasions hosted by the Pellatts, and the decorations combine the finest traditional details with the latest technology of the day.

The walls are lined with solid oak panels that took three German craftsmen three years to carve. The work in this room was so admired that it was first displayed in the Montreal Art Gallery before it was installed in the castle. There are a number of fine features in the carvings. Pheasants holding ribbons in their beaks are on either side of the central panel, and bunches of fruit and flowers extend down the sides of the panels.

The elaborate plaster ornamentation on the

*A side-board in the Oak Room.*

*Hand-carved panelling.*

*The Oak Room fireplace, showing a beautifully carved mantelpiece.*

ceiling was done by Italian craftsmen. In the centre is a great plaster oval originally illuminated by indirect lighting.

In the Pellatts' day this room had a Louis XVI carved and engraved imitation gold light standard that stood ten feet high. It was fitted with twenty-four electric bulbs designed to illuminate the many unique features of the room.

# THE STABLES

Casa Loma was not the first building that Sir Henry Pellatt constructed on this site. In 1906 he built a complex of structures, costing $250,000, which included the coach-house, greenhouse, potting shed, and stables. It also included the massive heating unit that would ultimately provide steam for the castle and all of the buildings.

The stable is a unique, romantic, fairy-tale building with a tall tower, turrets, impressive doors, and a golden-orange glazed tile roof. At different places the building has plaques, emblems, a statue of a squirrel eating nuts, lions, and the Pellatt coat of arms.

Inside, the stables are beautifully appointed. The stalls for the horses were made from Spanish mahogany, and over each horse stall hung the name of the occupant.

The walls are a creamy glazed tile imported from Spain. The floors are laid in a ribbed herring-bone pattern to give secure footing for the horses.

The carriage house, attached to the stables, is a vast room that held a number of automobiles and carriages in Pellatt's day. The floor is fourteen-inch-thick reinforced concrete able to take the heaviest of vehicles.

Originally the Casa Loma greenhouses were immediately to the south of the stables and attached to the potting shed. The Pellatts had half an acre under glass, where they grew a variety of indoor and outdoor plants. The greenhouse was taken down in the 1930s, and now the land is used as a small park, but the potting shed still stands and is used by the Casa Loma gardening staff.

*The interior of the Stables, showing the Spanish tile walls and the ribbed herring-bone pattern on the floor.*

# THE GARDENS

Sir Henry and Lady Mary loved
their gardens and won many
prizes for their plants and
flowers; however, in the years
after the Pellatts vacated
Casa Loma, the gardens went
completely wild.

In 1987 the Garden Club
of Toronto took over the task
of restoring the gardens with
the financial help of the city
and the Kiwanis Club.
When the club began its

work, a jungle of grapevines, some the size of cables, were strangling all other vegetation. Tons of plants were cut down and carted away.

Two dozen members of the club, all female volunteers, worked on the gardens with professional landscapers for five years before the grounds were restored. Today the gardens are maintained by the Casa Loma staff and are open to the public.

## Chapter 2
# FROM POVERTY TO PROSPERITY

Henry Mill Pellatt, born in Kingston on January 6, 1859, was a figure every bit as colourful as the castle he came to create. At the time of his birth, Upper Canada was an obscure backwater of the British Empire. Economic development was beginning to stir in the colony. The Grand Trunk Railway had been built between Windsor and Quebec City, and industries were starting to develop in cities, but most of the population eked out a living on marginal farms. Politically, Upper Canada and Lower Canada were locked in a stalemate as different factions vied for power in the legislature.

*EMILY   MINNIE   MOTHER   KATE*

*Henry's mother and three sisters in the 1870s.*

In the year of Henry's birth the Pellatt family was in the midst of a great crisis. Henry Pellatt Sr. had come to

*Henry Pellatt Sr.*

Canada in 1852, married Emma Holland, a native of Peterborough, and settled in Kingston. Henry Sr. had been trained in a bank in London, England, and he found employment at the Bank of Upper Canada. He was ambitious, and soon he became a stockbroker on the side and an agent in the liquor trade. However, by the time that Henry Jr. was born, his father was close to

bankruptcy. Bad management and an economic depression led to a downturn in the business. Debts mounted and creditors demanded to be paid. These difficulties were resolved only when Henry Sr. agreed to assign all of his meagre assets to his creditors.

**Early Toronto Days**

From this inauspicious beginning the fortunes of the Pellatts began to improve. To escape the reputation cast by their financial problems, the family moved to Toronto and Henry Sr. began work for another bank. In 1866 he established himself as a stockbroker with Edmund Osler, a member of a distinguished Toronto family. Soon the partnership of Pellatt and Osler was doing extremely well. By 1867 when Confederation united three of the British North American colonies into the independent Dominion of Canada, the Pellatt family had found new prosperity. They bought a home on Sherbourne Street, in one of the most prestigious neighbourhoods in the city, and Henry Jr., the oldest of a family that was to grow to be six children, was enrolled in the Model School, an élite educational institution.

Toronto, the largest centre in Ontario, expanded rapidly in the latter part of the nineteenth century. After Confederation it became the provincial capital and an important legislative and administrative centre, but it was also a commercial and manufacturing city. The financial industry became another important sector of Toronto's growing business community, and the Pellatt family was to play a prominent role in this area.

During Henry's childhood and up until the turn of the century, Toronto was predominantly a British city with strong links to the old country. Henry Pellatt Sr. was a royalist and an active member of the St. George's Society, which was dedicated to upholding the British Empire. Henry Jr. came to share those values from an early age and believed in them throughout his life.

*King Street in Toronto, about 1870.*

At school Henry was an adequate, if not outstanding, student, but he got a solid education at the Model School. He developed a reputation for his determination and desire to be first at everything, but it was in athletics that he excelled. He was a good lacrosse player and an exceptional long-distance runner.

In his last year of school Henry transferred to Upper Canada College. Then, just three months before his eighteenth birthday, he left school and went to work for his father's brokerage company, earning $16.60 a month. With his first pay cheque he bought a gold ring for his mother. He explained that it was a token of his love and esteem for her, but it was also an expression of the generosity that he was to display repeatedly in his life.

The partnership of Pellatt and Osler, located at 68

*Sir Edmund Osler.*

King Street East, was the centre of the increasingly active world of Toronto business. In 1876, the year Henry Jr. joined the firm, his father became the president of the Toronto Stock Exchange and remained in that position until 1880. The exchange in those days amounted to the activities of a group of traders who met in the back rooms of brokerage offices to buy and sell investment instruments. Henry Jr., an apprentice at the company, soon learned the art of trading and stock promotion that was to become the basis of his fortune.

## Young Man in a Hurry

But although he was now involved in a demanding business, Henry was not finished with his running career and began to train in earnest. His father complained that he was ignoring work, but Henry Jr. explained that he

*Henry poses in his racing costume, 1879.*
*Detail of one of Henry's medals.*

intended to set a new world record for the one-mile run. Once he had accomplished this, he promised his father he would quit racing and devote all of his time to business. He was true to his word.

In October 1878, Henry won the one-mile run in the Dominion championships, an annual Canadian event

held that year in Montreal. By 1879 he was at the top of his form. He won three important races in Toronto and then went to New York to race against a man who was so well known that the press referred to him simply as "Duffy." This race was sponsored by the National Association of Amateur Athletics and was run on a cinder track at the Mott Haven Athletic grounds in New York City.

Duffy was the unbeaten North American champion of the one-mile race. Track and field was a very popular sport at that time, and thousands of people came to watch the race between the veteran and the young Canadian challenger, Henry Pellatt. From the start of the race Henry took the lead. Two other runners were forced to quit by the third lap because of the blistering pace. Still Duffy tried to close the gap. This is how a newspaper of the day described it:

> Amidst the most intense excitement both runners finished the fourth lap almost neck and neck and commenced the fifth and last lap together. Round they went, Duffy gaining a few inches, but it was evident he was to be beaten and amidst the yells of thousands they dashed into the straight, one hundred yards from home. Our Canadian was evidently not aware that Duffy was really so close, but both men were at their best and they fought it out to the tape ... [Pellatt] winning by two feet and beating the hitherto undefeated one miler of New York.

Henry had set a new world record of four minutes, forty-two and two-fifths seconds. This is not a particularly fast time by today's standards, but the race reflects Pellatt's single-minded determination. Here was a man who set himself a goal and focused on it until it was accomplished. This quality would serve him well in his later life. And as he had promised his father, once he set the record he quit racing and dedicated himself to his business career.

## Rifleman Pellatt

Another lifelong activity began in 1876. In that year Henry joined the Queen's Own Rifles of Canada as a rifleman. The Queen's Own, named for Queen Victoria, was the largest militia unit in the country. In some ways

*Captain and Brevet-Major Henry Mill Pellatt, 1883.*

One particular story reflects Pellatt's approach. When Henry first joined the unit, he had some difficulty learning the drill. In his forthright manner he hired an officer to come over to his home in the evening to give him private lessons. Soon he not only mastered the art of the drill but was teaching the officer the proper procedures.

Henry's first and only active military engagement was in 1877, when the Queen's Own Rifles was ordered to Belleville, Ontario, to deal with striking railroad workers. There had been a serious recession in the mid-1870s, and the Grand Trunk Railway laid off some workers and reduced the wages of other employees to deal with this crisis. The workers responded by going on strike on December 29, 1876. The mayor and magistrate of Belleville, fearing that the civil authorities would be completely overwhelmed, asked for military assistance. The Queen's Own Rifles agreed to provide it. No one, it seems, questioned the appropriateness of using the military against a civilian population involved in a labour dispute.

Early in the morning of January 2, 1877, 167 officers and men of the Queen's Own, including young rifleman Henry Pellatt, mustered in Toronto, and by 10:30 a.m. they were dispatched by train to Belleville. When the force arrived, they were met by an angry mob of several hundred strikers and their supporters. The mood soon turned ugly. The mob threw rocks, ice balls, bolts, and anything else they could get their hands on at the military men. The soldiers were ordered to fix bayonets and advance on the crowd. Fortunately no one was seriously injured. One man was wounded with a bayonet in the thigh, and another received a stomach injury. Soon the threatening situation subsided, and by 7:00 a.m. the next morning the soldiers withdrew, taking their casualties with them: two soldiers with head injuries from flying rocks, three with frozen feet, and several with frozen fingers.

It was an engagement that tells much about the political role of the military at that time. The militia was an institution dedicated to the defence of

the unit was more of a club than a military force; its members were part-time soldiers who met in the evenings and on the weekends. They drilled, did military exercises, and dressed up for ceremonial occasions. Most of the costs of running the regiment were borne by the men themselves.

Pellatt was an enthusiastic supporter of the militia. He attended events as often as business permitted and got tremendous enjoyment out of the fraternity of his fellow officers and men. As in all of his activities, once Pellatt made a commitment to the Queen's Own, he became involved with single-minded dedication to be the best and to contribute to the utmost of his abilities.

constituted authority and the status quo. The members were strong supporters of a British Canada within the empire, and they were proud to be dedicated royalists. The soldiers involved in the incident received medals made from the rails torn up by the strikers, and Pellatt proudly wore his at fancy-dress military occasions for the rest of his life.

*Lady Mary Pellatt's fan.*

Henry Pellatt loved the pomp and ceremony of the military as well as the elaborate mess dinners and serious socializing, but he also identified with those conservative political values that members of militia supported. However, Pellatt had another reason to be active with the Queen's Own Rifles: it was good for business. His involvement with the regiment increased the number of people that he met and gave him access to a widening social set in Toronto, in Canada, and in Great Britain. All of these connections would be useful in his future business ventures.

In the late 1870s and early 1880s, Henry Pellatt was a young dandy who liked to parade along King Street wearing lavender trousers and sporting long sideburns. He had travelled to Britain and Continental Europe. He was tall, handsome, affable, with a large number of friends and a promising business career. Obviously he was a very eligible bachelor.

His single status did not last long. When he was twenty-three, in June 1882, he married Mary Dodgson, who was two years his senior. Her father had died when Mary was still young, but her mother had managed to send her to Bishop Strachan School, the leading Anglican institution for girls. Henry had known her for some years before they were married. He no doubt found her English family background and social graces compatible with his own,

but what he talked about was her beauty and the grace of her neck. Henry was practical in life and romantic in his sensibilities.

The couple was a study in contrasts. While Henry was a man who loved social occasions and who sought prominence, Mary was shy and retiring. She was his constant companion and support through their life, but she liked to remain in the background. Once the couple returned from their honeymoon in Europe, they bought a house at 559 Sherbourne Street, not far from both sets of parents. Three years later, in 1885, the couple's only child, Reginald, was born.

## Pellatt the Plunger

Shortly after the marriage, Pellatt Sr. felt Henry was ready to become fully engaged in the family business. In 1882 the Osler-Pellatt partnership broke up, and on March 1, 1883, Henry Pellatt Sr. formally set up partner-

*Detail from Lady Pellatt's Suite.*

ship with his son under the name of Pellatt and Pellatt. At the age of twenty-four, young Henry was a full partner in one of the most active brokerage companies in Canada.

He was to make his mark in business very quickly. In the 1880s electricity was the newest scientific marvel. Thomas Edison developed a method to generate electric power from steam-driven turbines and invented an inexpensive light-bulb. French, German, British, and American inventors developed commercially viable methods to provide illumination for cities, and power to drive trolley cars and machinery in industry. Henry was very excited about this new technology, and although his father was deeply skeptical, the young businessman established the Toronto Electric Light Company in 1883, the first electric company in the city, with $125,000 capital from Canadian and English investors. Pellatt became the company secretary with a salary of twenty-five dollars a month.

*Toronto in the 1890s was growing rapidly.*

Many people in those days were very concerned about the safety of electricity. Because electric power was transmitted by cable, it seemed somehow mysterious and dangerous to many. Some even believed that it was a "grave danger to horses and drivers." Soon, however, the company received a contract from the City of Toronto to provide thirty-two street lights, and gained three other private customers. With these contracts the company built a steam-generating plant that consumed a half a ton of coal a night. The real success for the company came in 1889, when it negotiated a thirty-year monopoly to provide street lighting to the city.

Pellatt's first major financial windfall, however, came with speculation in the Canada North West Land

Company. Edmund Osler, Pellatt Sr.'s former partner, established this company in 1882 to acquire and sell five million acres of land on the Canadian prairies that had been granted to the Canadian Pacific Railway as part of the payment for building the rail line through to the west coast. Investors were reluctant to support the North West Land Company. In the 1880s there was little confidence in the Canadian west. Settlement was slow and many felt the land could not sustain agriculture. Stock in the company languished.

Young Henry travelled across to the west coast shortly after the railway was completed and came back an enthusiastic booster of the prairies and the project. He set out to buy every share of the North West Land Company that he could lay his hands on. Most of his shares were bought for between twelve and fourteen dollars each. Other investors remained skeptical and ridiculed the rash speculation. "Pellatt the Plunger" was the snide label Henry earned from his colleagues. But that was not to last for long. The value of the shares of the company floated upwards until they were worth more than ninety dollars each by the 1890s. Henry Pellatt realized between $3 million and $4 million on his investment (more than $100 million today). Pellatt the Plunger was now a man of prosperity.

## Chapter 3

# PELLATT THE PROMOTER

By the 1880s young Henry Pellatt had become a promoter and financier of companies. His method of operation was simple: he would see a business opportunity, form a company, and finance it by raising money from investors. He would stay involved in the affairs of the company by becoming a member of the board of directors, often its chair, and then, once the share prices had risen, he would take his profits by selling his shares. It seems like a simple strategy, but it took business savvy and, above all, good contacts.

## The Finance Capitalist

Pellatt became a finance capitalist in the era when the financier governed the commanding heights of the economy. Prior to World War I there was a great need for capital to pay for the massive projects of the day. Railroads, smelters, mines, utilities, and a wide variety of manufacturing enterprises from textiles to farm machinery were all built using money raised by finance capitalists.

Financiers such as J.P. Morgan in the United States and the Rothschilds in England and Europe came to have immense power and wealth because of their ability to raise capital and

*George Cox.*

*A.E. Ames.*

to finance projects. The centre of capital markets at that time was Europe, particularly London, and the money for many Canadian projects came from Britain. That was one of the major reasons why the financial and business élite of this country valued its connection to the British Empire.

Montreal was the largest financial centre in Canada at that time, but Toronto was rapidly developing as a source of funds for projects in Ontario and the West. There were a number of key players in Toronto such as George Cox, president of the Bank of Commerce, and A.E. Ames, Cox's son-in-law, who owned and ran a brokerage house. Pellatt and Pellatt was another important brokerage firm in the city, and, using the company as a base, Henry developed an extensive network of contacts in the business community in Toronto, in Canada, and in Europe.

The financial markets of that day were largely unregulated and shady practices were so common that even established businesspeople frequently denounced all stock markets as little more than gambling dens.

*A Toronto stockbroker's office, about 1910.*

Syndicates would be formed to inflate the price of stocks, insider trading was common, and dishonest news, extolling the prospects of a company, would be released for the sole purpose of inflating the price of its stock. Often the financiers who controlled these companies would divert the money of the investors for their own personal use, or they would drive up the debt of the companies to the point of ruin while they paid themselves handsome profits.

In this type of an environment, where fraud was commonplace, it was essential for the successful promoter to convince prospective investors that his deals were honest. Henry Pellatt understood this better than most, and self-promotion, as a way to build confidence in his deals, became part of his business strategy.

Henry promoted himself in different ways. Every time his name was associated with the Queen's Own Rifles (and during this period Pellatt rapidly moved up through the officer ranks), his stature would increase. Every time he met royalty, his name would be mentioned in "proper social circles." Every time he had a business success or made a generous donation to a charity, it added to the perception that he was a successful and honest businessman. All of these activities made potential investors believe that he was a wealthy man whose ventures were bound to be profitable.

This is not to say that Pellatt did not engage in sharp practices himself. He made a great deal of money on the Toronto Stock Exchange, a place known at that time for stock manipulations and questionable deals. In 1897, for example, fifteen Toronto brokers were charged with false advertising. These brokers represented all of the large brokerage companies, Pellatt and Pellatt included. All charges were ultimately dismissed, but such an incident does suggest the type of practices that were common, and Pellatt was at the centre of the Toronto exchange.

*Henry Pellatt Sr., his wife, and children.*

## From Prosperity to Wealth

In 1892, when Pellatt was thirty-three, his father retired and Henry Jr. was given full reign to run the company as he saw fit. He brought Norman Macrae into the firm, and they remained partners for the rest of Pellatt's career. It was a good arrangement: Macrae was a conservative businessman who was content to look after the day-to-day affairs of the company, leaving Henry free to promote his many business activities, find investors, and pursue his military, social, and philanthropic activities.

Pellatt had become a success in a fairly difficult business climate. Granted, he had an enormous advantage because he was able to use his father's company, which already had an established reputation, as the base for his business activities. But the period between 1873 and 1896 was one of economic stagnation for Canada. Business confidence was low, and generally prices were on a downward slide. The Canadian Pacific Railway was built through to the west coast, but it did not spur much growth. Those immigrants who came into the country frequently left to go to the United States, along with many native-born Canadians. Economic growth was slow, the population remained relatively stable, and many people felt that Canada would never be more than a wintry outpost of the British Empire.

All of that suddenly changed in 1896, when economic prosperity arrived so quickly and dramatically that few could comprehend it. Canada at last seemed to be on the road to growth that had so long eluded it. In that year the new Liberal government of Wilfrid Laurier was elected and claimed credit for this prosperity. The Liberals were hardly the sole reason, but they did have the political adroitness to manage the growth in an imaginative way.

Clifford Sifton, the minister of the Interior, began to actively promote economic growth by advocating that the country's natural resources should be exploited. Immigration was the key, he felt, and he promoted settlement in Canada across Europe. Soon a flood of immigrants began to pour in from countries such as Britain, Poland, the Ukraine, Russia, Lithuania, the Scandinavian countries, Italy, Serbia, Romania, and others. In time these immigrants came to change the whole character of Canada.

Many of these people took up homesteads on the prairies. Others provided cheap labour for industries in rapidly growing cities. They helped to build two new railways through to the west coast, and provided the bulk of the labour in the mines of Northern Ontario and British Columbia. Economic expansion was dramatic. There was a feeling of buoyancy in the air. Foreign loans and investments were pouring into the country. New towns were springing up. Wages began to rise, exports increased, and farm production, particularly of wheat in the West, grew rapidly. Despite inflation there was an increase in the standard of living. Rags-to-riches stories were commonplace.

This was a perfect opportunity for a promoter such as Henry Pellatt. The period even seemed to reflect his expansive, optimistic personality. With the growing economy, companies made record profits while expanding swiftly. The optimism made it much easier to find money for new projects. Investors wanted to be in at the ground floor of these ventures, and Henry, as the president of one of the most active brokerage companies in Toronto, was at the centre of much of this action.

Pellatt's business interests included a great range of activities. He was on the boards of two life insurance companies: Manufacturers Life and Empire Life. He played a leading role in the establishment of Brazilian Traction, a company that operates today under the name of Brascan, and remains a major Canadian multinational corporation. He had a big interest in the Lake and Ocean Navigation Company (later renamed Canada Steamship Lines), which owned steamships, one of which was named the *Pellatt*. He had major stock holdings in both the Grand Trunk Pacific Railway and the Canadian Pacific Railway. He was on the board of the Toronto Street Railway and the Home Bank of Canada. Pellatt was the director of a score of mining companies. He was instrumental in forming the Crow's Nest Coal Company in British Columbia and also became a director of Dominion Steel Corporation and Dominion Coal Company.

*A group inspecting the hydro power project in Niagara Falls. Henry is the fifth from the right.*

By the end of the first decade of the twentieth century Henry Pellatt had become fabulously wealthy. All together, he sat on the boards of at least one hundred companies and was the chair or president of more than twenty. His net worth was estimated to be $17 million (approximately $485 million today). Granted, most of this was tied up in stocks and bonds that he could not easily access, but there was no doubt that he was a fantastically wealthy man by any standard.

## Electric Power for the People

Pellatt had a special interest in electric power since he had first helped to establish the Toronto Electric Light Company in 1883. This company had expanded rapidly, and by the end of the 1890s it had 175 miles of wire strung up through the city, 550 street lights, and a number of private customers. Once alternating current was developed, by the Westinghouse Company, it was possible to transport electric power over long distances. A group of Americans in the early 1890s built the first large-scale generating station at Niagara Falls and provided power for streetcars, electric light, and industry. Pellatt and others began looking for a way to exploit the falls.

In 1903 Pellatt's Toronto Electric Light Company joined with William Mackenzie of the Toronto Railway Company and Frederic Nicholls of the Canadian General Electric Company to form a syndicate to bring power from Niagara to Toronto. This group was given the exclusive right by the Ontario government to take water from the Niagara River, at Tempest Point, to generate electrical power and build transmission lines to Toronto. Pellatt became the president of the organization, the Electrical Development Company of Ontario.

This was a very profitable deal for the members of the syndicate. For an investment of $30,000, they incorporated a company with a capital stock of $6 million and with a potential stock value worth several times that amount once the scheme was accepted by the public. Soon the stock increased in value

*Frederic Nicholls.*

*Pellatt, with other dignitaries, at the laying of the cornerstone at the site of the Electrical Development Company's power plant in Niagara Falls.*

as shareholders clamoured to get into the deal. Now the syndicate's holdings were in the millions. This was called stock watering, a common practice in that era.

The project was a major engineering feat, given the construction techniques of the day, and required a huge amount of capital. To begin the financing the syndicate agreed to raise $5 million by issuing 30-year bonds at 5 per cent interest. The funds were quickly raised and the construction went ahead.

From the beginning there was considerable public opposition to the granting of this concession. Populists and Reformers denounced it as a give-away of public resources to monopoly interests. Gradually the assault on the Pellatt, Mackenzie, and Nicholls syndicate mounted, and the demand for the public ownership of utilities grew in popularity.

*Sir Adam Beck.*

The leader of the fight for publicly owned electric power came to be Adam Beck, a Conservative member of the Ontario legislature, former Mayor of London, and a manufacturer of fine veneers. When the Conservatives came to power in 1905, under the leadership of Whitney, Beck dedicated himself to the fight both inside and outside government.

The public debate on this issue was intense. Municipalities hosted rallies and public meetings on the question, and Beck, a brilliant public speaker, drew huge crowds to hear him argue passionately for public ownership. Every day the issue was on the front pages of the newspapers. Beck lobbied hard to move the issue forward within government and in 1906 the Hydro Electric Commission of Ontario was established.

As the public fight continued, the syndicate found themselves in a weak position. Their existing utility companies were said to provide poor service at high cost. The public fear was that they would use their monopoly position to charge high rates at the expense of the customer and ignore unprofitable markets that were expensive to service.

Pellatt's syndicate counterattacked by claiming that public ownership was despotism, would ruin Canadian credit, and even that it was unconstitutional. Pellatt, Mackenzie, Nicholls, and others made speeches defending free enterprise and their right to develop their company, but little attention was given to them because they obviously had vested interests in this issue. Desperate to get their point of view heard in the debate, they paid for letters, articles, and editorials to appear in newspapers, and even went so far as to offer $350,000 to *The World*, a Toronto newspaper that was the strongest supporter of the public utilities, if it would change its position. When this became known the public became even more hostile to their cause.

The syndicate tried to shoulder through this controversy, but it was increasingly difficult. It became impossible to sell company bonds to raise the capital needed to continue with the construction program because investors feared that they could lose all of their money if the government nationalized the company. It appeared for a time that the entire program would come to an end.

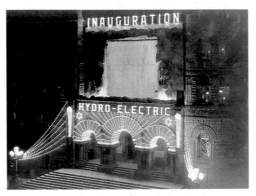

*Toronto City Hall, decorated for the inauguration of hydro-electric power, 1911.*

Finally William Mackenzie took the lead in finding a solution. In 1908, after a complicated series of manoeuvres, he consolidated a number of railways and then purchased the Electrical Development Company from other members of the syndicate. In 1911 Pellatt sold out his remaining interests in other electrical companies to him.

This appeared to be a brilliant move. Mackenzie had created a self-contained group of companies that generated, transmitted, and consumed electric power, but it still was not able to withstand the onslaught of Adam Beck, the "human dynamo," and the campaign for public ownership. In 1910 the Ontario Hydro-Electric Power Commission switched on power to the city of Berlin (later renamed Kitchener), and in

*Sir Henry, shown here in 1905 (back seat), had a large collection of carriages and automobiles.*

1911 power was switched on in Toronto itself, to a cheering crowd of forty thousand to fifty thousand people. Rapidly the public company was taking over the markets of the private electricity producers. Finally in 1920 the commission bought Mackenzie's power generating and transmitting companies, and virtually all of the power companies in the province were publicly owned. Ontario Hydro, today the largest publicly owned

corporation in North America, had been born.

This fight was the most important, but not the only, challenge to the group of financiers who dominated Toronto business in the first decade of the twentieth century. The 1906 federal Royal Commission on Life Insurance Companies showed that they practised fast and loose investment policies for their own benefit. The group controlled the life insurance companies and frequently used the money of policy holders to fund their own projects. Often they ignored the rules of conflict of interest and frequently practised blatant nepotism. Pellatt was a director of Manufacturers' Life and sat on its investment committee. He was specifically named in this inquiry as having used money from the policies of small investors as a source of funds for his utility and stock promotions without the approval of the committee.

Nothing was done about the findings of this commission because it could not be shown that anyone was harmed by these practices, but increasingly the public demanded that something be done to reign in the power of this group of wealthy businessmen. The Toronto financial group defended themselves by proclaiming their personal integrity, and Henry Pellatt was insulted that his honesty was being questioned. The group could not appreciate that the public viewed them as arrogant, ignoring the public good and making excessive profits. Difficulties were gathering but Pellatt and other financiers continued on as if their world would never change.

## Chapter 4

# THE BUSINESS OF SOLDIERING

*This photograph, showing Culloden House on Sherbourne Street about 1890, gives a sense of the grandeur of the Pellatts' neighbourhood.*

As Henry Pellatt gained prominence with his business activities, one of the ways he kept his name in the forefront was through his involvement with the Queen's Own Rifles. By 1895 he was promoted to the rank of full major, and in 1897 he accompanied the Canadian contingent to the Diamond Jubilee of Queen Victoria. While at the celebrations he was appointed to command the Colonial Guard of Honour for the Queen in front of St. Paul's Cathedral. For his efforts he was given an autographed photograph of the Queen. He cherished it for the rest of his life.

## Social Life of the Pellatts

By the late 1890s Henry and his wife Mary were at the centre of a fashionable, if rather formal and stuffy, social set of Toronto's leading citizens. The Pellatts had a handsome home on Sherbourne Street and received guests at their Cliffside cottage in Scarborough every Saturday.

Always dressed immaculately, they were a substantial, attractive couple. Henry is described by Carlie Oreskovich, his biographer, as being "a compendium of characters of everything from kindly paternalism through to shrewdness and military severity." He had a well-trimmed moustache, and his receding hairline and sleepy eyes made him appear aloof and remote. His wife Mary wore full dresses flowing down to her ankles, as was the style of the day. She fancied big brimmed hats often decorated with artificial flowers and frequently carried a parasol.

Towards the middle part of his life Henry lost his athletic figure and ballooned up to three hundred pounds. Often when guests arrived, he would eat a modest meal, and later, when everyone else had retired, he would visit the kitchen, where the cook had another meal waiting for him. But in his military uniforms he looked magnificent. All of his clothes were tailored to fit him perfectly and kept in the best condition. His added girth seemed to give him a more substantial military bearing, helping him to look like a leader in every way.

## Colonel Sir Henry Pellatt

In 1901 Pellatt was promoted over the heads of a number of others to be made the commanding officer of the Queen's Own Rifles, and given the rank of colonel. He was delighted with this promotion, and he had enough money to play the role with a flourish. This afforded him the chance to host elaborate mess dinners, and he was given the opportunity to organize large-scale military events. Even more important than this, his connection to the regiment gave him added prestige and provided him with the opportunity to be associated with the "top rank" of British and Canadian society and to raise capital for his companies.

In October of that year Pellatt organized eleven thousand military personnel, drawn from a number of units across Canada, to honour a visit from the Duke and Duchess of Cornwall and York at the Canadian National Exhibition grounds. The Duke (later to become King George V) borrowed Henry's favourite horse, Prince, a fine-looking dapple white stallion, to parade at the event. There were military bands, a march past in full dress uniform by the troops, and other ceremonies. It was estimated that 250,000 people turned out to watch this event, almost as many people as lived in the city at that time.

As his contribution to the celebration of the visit, Pellatt provided thirty-five hundred electric lights for a city hall reception for the Duke

*Lady Mary Pellatt, about 1900.*

*Bay Street, showing an archway constructed in honour of the visit of the Duke and Duchess of Cornwall and York, 1901.*

and Duchess. This was an expensive but shrewd investment for the promoter. It was a highly public display of electric power, and one of his companies held the monopoly on the delivery of electricity in the city. More important, it was a display of Pellatt's wealth that increased his stature with royalty and the public at large. For a man such as Henry, who aspired to royal recognition, it was money well spent.

There were other displays of Pellatt's generosity and opportunities to be involved in the military pageantry that he loved so much. In 1902 he headed the Canadian military contingent to the coronation of Edward VII. He also brought the Queen's Own bugle band, at his own expense, to play at the coronation. He covered some costs of the regiment and gave away a substantial amount of money to charity. Honours came his way. He was appointed the aide-de-camp to the governor general, Lord Albert Grey, but still he wanted more.

In 1904 Pellatt appealed to the minister of the Militia, Frederick William Borden, for help in getting the recognition he so craved. At first Borden offered him the title of companion of St. Michael and George, but this was not adequate. Pellatt appealed to the minister to be named a knight bachelor. As he stated in a letter, this would be the preferred honour because "it will give me a better standing for business purposes."

Borden agreed to recommend him, and, following protocol, Governor General Grey made the recommendation. The following is part of the citation by the governor general.

*Sir Henry on his favourite charger, Prince.*

Colonel Pellatt holds a high social position at Toronto, is one of the most enterprising businessmen in the Dominion and has spent considerable sums of money in his efforts to bring the regiment under his command ... up to the highest possible standard of efficiency. Owing to Colonel Pellatt's exertions this Regiment has the greatest of any in Canada and has the reputation of being the smartest also.

On November 8, 1905, it was announced that Pellatt had been awarded to the order of knight bachelor. From that day forward he would be called Sir Henry Mill Pellatt, or simply Sir Henry. His wife would be known as Lady Mary. He would long remember this as his greatest honour and finest hour. Congratulations poured in from associates in business and military circles from Canada, Britain, and the United States. He was deeply touched.

## To Aldershot for the Empire

This award seemed to stir Sir Henry to even greater displays of wealth and generosity. In 1906 he took the full complement of the Queen's Own Rifles, 891 men all together, to New York City for a military tournament arranged by the Twelfth Regiment of New York. Sir Henry paid the entire regimental costs for this trip.

The year 1910, however, marked the high point of Pellatt's generosity with the regiment. That year was the fiftieth anniversary of the founding of the Queen's Own Rifles, and Sir Henry was determined to mark it in grand style. Every night for an entire week in the month of June, the regiment and the Pellatts put on a two-hour, extravagant pageant at the stadium at the Exhibition grounds that involved twelve hundred people, two military bands, pipers, four hundred schoolchildren, scenery, and the re-enactment of the high points of Canadian history.

The pageant was a romantic interpretation of history with, not surprisingly, a special emphasis on the role of the military. As Oreskovich explained, it began with the arrival of Loyalists from 1789, then moved to the

*This flattering drawing of Sir Henry was published in* The World, *an English magazine, on the occasion of his Aldershot visit.*

… defense of Canada, the Fenian raids, the Riel Rebellion, and concluded with an extravagant scene that featured no less a regal figure than King George V on horseback proceeded by an impressive cast of historical characters including Henry VII, Queen Elizabeth of York, Anne Boleyn, Jane Seymour, Sir Walter Raleigh, Shakespeare, Oliver Cromwell, James II, Bonnie Prince Charlie, George Washington and even Napoleon Bonaparte.

The battle scenes were punctuated with flashes from the muzzles of guns and clouds of smoke. At one point the schoolchildren, dressed in red, white, and blue, arranged themselves to form a Union Jack. As they sang patriotic songs, they waved miniature Union Jack flags to the applause of the audience. Sir Henry paid the estimated $25,000 cost of the event, and his electric company provided brilliant illumination with thousands of electric lights.

The Toronto press loved the spectacle and praised Sir Henry. There was some comment that perhaps Canadian history had not been quite as militaristic as the pageant portrayed, but that seemed a minor criticism. Many felt this was just the sort of history that schoolchildren should be learning about. A "superb historical kindergarten of intense dramatic and educational interest," one newspaper called it.

A group of Native people from the Six Nations

*Sir Henry as Chief Tawyunansara, 1910.*

Reserve took part in the pageant by performing a war dance. After performing for a garden party, these Native people, in full war paint and regalia, suddenly surrounded a startled Sir Henry. One performer gave a short speech and concluded by bestowing him with the honour of a Native name, "Tawyunansara" (the Dawn of the Morning). They then placed on him a brilliant headdress and stole of eagle feathers, satin, and coloured stones. Sir Henry was obviously embarrassed, but it was another honour he could not refuse. Lady Mary laughed so hard she could hardly contain herself.

The pageant's finale was a formal regimental ball sponsored and paid for by Sir Henry, the commanding officer of the Queen's Own, and held in the Transportation Building of the Exhibition grounds. It was a grand affair. The hall was decorated with flags and bunting. Sir Henry, dressed in his ceremonial dark green uniform, and Lady Pellatt, in a cream brocade gown trimmed with Brussels lace, with a diamond pendant and gold crown, led the couples around the floor in a grand march to the Queen's Own regimental tune. It was like a moment from another age when good manners, courtly gestures, and formal clothes were all that was important.

In 1910 Sir Henry also sponsored an event that was more spectacular than anything he had previously undertaken. Pellatt took 640 men of the Queen's Own Rifles to Aldershot, England,

*Sir Henry and the Queen's Own Rifles outside Guildhall, 1910.*

for seven weeks of military manoeuvres and paid for the entire trip out of his own funds. Both the British and the Canadians were stunned at the extravagance. It was estimated to have cost him at least a quarter of a million dollars. No one had made such a grand gesture since Lord Strathcona sent a regiment to fight in the Boer War.

There was a grand send-off starting from the armories on University Avenue with speeches from Sir Henry and Lady Mary, a march down to Union Station with excited

*Sir Henry receives the title of Commander of the Royal Victorian Order, Third Class, from the future King George V at Balmoral Castle, 1910.*

crowds lining the street, the long trip to England, military manoeuvres in Aldershot, training with British regular troops for six weeks, and the trip back to Canada.

In the midst of the activities Sir Henry and the senior officers were invited to Balmoral Castle to meet the future King George V and receive commendation as the first colonial regiment to cross the ocean and take part in manoeuvres in the mother country. Sir Henry was given the added title of commander of the Royal Victorian Order, third class. There were speeches about the empire while Sir Henry spoke about "our deep and abiding loyalty to your Majesty and to our gracious Queen."

In four years many of the men who had crossed to Europe with Pellatt were to return again to fight in the Great War. The Queen's Own Rifles sent 210 officers and 7,352 men overseas in the war. In total 1,254 of them were to die in the conflict.

*Sir Henry leads the troops at Aldershot.*

## Chapter 5

# THE CASTLE ON THE HILL

Sir Henry and Lady Pellatt lived in a style that few Canadians could ever attain. They owned a magnificent home on Sherbourne Street, the most fashionable area of the city. Their friends were drawn from the social, military, business, and political elite of Toronto, Canada, and the British Empire, and they had enough money to buy anything they desired. This lifestyle was fit for anyone of substance, but it was not enough for Sir Henry.

### Dreams of Grandeur

In the period from 1880 to 1914 the wealthy of North America built private mansions on a scale never seen before or since. Some have called it the "Gilded Age of the Vanderbilts" after the family whose private homes came to epitomize this movement. Clusters of extravagant houses were built in Newport, Rhode Island; in Southampton, on Long Island; and along the Hudson River and on the Thousand Islands, in Upper New York State; winter retreats were built along the beaches in Florida and California. Mansions were also built by the wealthy in the cities and suburbs across the continent.

*Benvenuto, shown here in 1909, was the home of Sir William Mackenzie.*

These huge, expensive houses were built as visible symbols of power and wealth and as backdrops for lavish dinners, parties, and balls with liveried servants, exotic foods, drinks, and music. These homes were built using modern construction techniques, but many hearkened back, in architectural style, to French châteaux, palaces of Italian merchant princes, or English manor-houses. These families were able to afford such mansions because of the fantastic fortunes that they acquired during this era, but as well, there was no income tax or business tax and wages for labour and servants were very low.

For years Sir Henry had nurtured the dream of having a grand home of his own. He was a man who loved the big gesture, and he wanted a house where he could live in a style appropriate for his position and for the entertainment of business associates and others he wanted to impress. Above all he dreamed of a house like some of the grand castles of Europe that could be the residence of the royal family when they were in Toronto.

In the first decade of the twentieth century Sir Henry Pellatt was making more money than he could spend. Granted,

*Ardwold, shown here in about 1910, was the home of Sir John and Lady Eaton.*

Not even this scare could dampen Sir Henry's dream of building a spectacular new home. In 1903 Henry (he was not knighted until 1905) and his wife Mary visited a piece of property just outside the city limits on top of Davenport Hill. It was a magnificent site. The crest of the hill was six hundred feet above the level of Lake Ontario. From there they could look out on the developing city of Toronto, which lay at their feet, and see the lake in the distance. The property extended north from Davenport Road and contained about fifteen acres of land and eight building lots.

The couple were convinced that this land would be the perfect site for the dramatic house that they aspired to build. Both of them were very excited about the prospect. Henry purchased the property, putting it in the name of his wife. At Mary Pellatt's suggestion they adopted the name of Casa Loma, Spanish for "House on the Hill," a name that had already been given to the property by a former owner.

Pellatt had turned his business interests to property development in those days, and he began to speculate on land in the immediate area. In 1905 he bought a parcel of land that was the private golf course of his neighbour Albert Austin, who lived in nearby Spadina House, and in 1908 he purchased another section of land in the area south of St. Clair Avenue West and Bathurst Street. The Pellatt parcel now stretched from Davenport Road in the south to St. Clair in the north and from Bathurst Street to Spadina Road.

Part of this property was subdivided into sixty-eight lots and put up for sale. Later Sir Henry would state that

there were suggestions that the foundations of his fortune might not be secure. In 1907 there was a stock market panic. Sir Henry had borrowed heavily to go into investments, using his stocks as security. His stocks fell, and he could not cover the payments on the loans. The banks began to sell his stocks to cover their position. Soon there was the fear that this would drive down the price of the securities and that many people would be hurt financially.

A group of investors met to try and develop a strategy to deal with the crisis. Through it all Sir Henry was calm. One morning the group arrived early, expecting to have to make some difficult decisions. Pellatt kept them waiting for hours. When he finally did appear, he was carefree and well rested. "Sorry to be so late," he told them, "but you fellows kept me up so dashed long last night I overslept." Whether this was supreme confidence or lack of appreciation of the seriousness of the situation is not known, but Pellatt's actions did seem to give new resolve to the group. The bankers and investors rallied to his support, and the value of Pellatt's holdings floated upwards again.

the sale of these lots was going slowly and that he conceived of the plan to build Casa Loma as an anchor to spur this development. He claimed that he made a profit of $1 million, over and above the cost of building Casa Loma, but this seems highly unlikely. The total money received from the sale of the lots was nowhere close to $1 million, let alone sufficient to cover the cost of the building. But Pellatt was intent on building a grand house regardless of the cost or consequences.

## Designing the Dream

Sir Henry engaged his good friend E.J. Lennox, the architect who had worked on the powerhouse at Niagara Falls, to design the buildings on the Casa Loma property. The two businessmen were well suited to each other. Lennox had grand dreams of his own and the drive to realize them. He was the architect of Toronto's Old City Hall, which was completed in 1898, and a number of other important buildings in the city. One difficulty was that Lennox was a perfectionist and insisted on using only the best materials. This drove up the costs, but that was no problem for Sir Henry. He had deep pockets, and costs were not a consideration.

The first thing the pair did was to travel to Europe in 1905 to study different types of buildings and develop a design for the new house. Pellatt knew clearly what he wanted: a grand and imposing structure that showed strong classical and medieval influences and that was still modern and convenient. This is how he later described it:

*E.J. Lennox, the architect of Casa Loma.*

All my life I have been a student of architecture, and I have traveled extensively in England, Scotland, Ireland, Germany, Austria and Italy. I had the opportunity to observe and carefully examine many ancient fortresses and castles. Casa Loma is a result of my observations and travels.

On their European travels, Lennox made hundreds of sketches of the grand buildings they visited while Sir Henry looked at furnishings.

The massive castle at the top of the hill was not the first building that they constructed on the property. In 1906 they set to work on the stables, greenhouses, potting shed, and coach-house, which was located at the northwest corner of Walmer Road and Austin Terrace. A huge coal and steam heating plant, which consumed eight hundred tons of coal a year, was built almost immediately under the potting shed. The cost of this complex was approximately $250,000.

The stables are an odd fantasy building with towers and turrets, and statues of lions, lemmings, and heraldic figures, as well as the Pellatt coat of arms, which Sir Henry had recently acquired. The stalls for the horses were made of Spanish mahogany, and over each stall was the name of an animal in gold leaf lettering. The floor was fourteen-inch-thick reinforced concrete and contained enough room for twenty horses, a collection of carriages, sleighs, and automobiles. The walls were covered in glazed cream tile, and the floor tile was set in a ribbed

*The gardens at Casa Loma today.*

herringbone pattern to prevent the horses from slipping.

The Pellatts loved gardening and were fond of displaying plants and flowers at every possible occasion. The greenhouses were removed many years ago, but they originally stood immediately to the south of the stables and covered half an acre. A full-time gardener and his staff worked to provide plants for the estate. There was a large fruit and vegetable garden that sat across the street from the greenhouse and stables, and that extended all the way from Austin Terrace to a point one hundred yards north of the stables. At other places on the property there were cages with Canada geese, pheasants, owls, and poultry. Pellatt kept a cow to produce fresh dairy products for his table, and there was a paddock that contained elk and several deer.

The coach-house, or "Hunting Lodge," as it was later called, is in fact a substantial, two-storey brick building with servants quarters and an octagonal sun room facing south. Once this complex was complete, Sir Henry sold or gave his Scarborough summer home to his son, Reginald, and began to use the coach-house as his summer residence. Often he

would bring friends, business associates, and officers from the regiment up to his new estate to visit the gardens, ride horses, watch the work in progress, or simply relax.

E.J. Lennox had been working on the ideas for the castle since 1906, but he did not begin the serious design stage until September 1909. Sir Henry had considerable influence on the plans for the final building. He wanted it to look like an imposing castle fit for a military man such as him. He planned to turn Casa Loma into the largest military museum in the Western Hemisphere, and he ensured that the floors were strong enough to carry heavy military equipment. However, the ideas of Lennox are pervasive in the building.

There are many different influences in the design from Norman to English, French, Irish, Italian, and German. Lennox called it "French Baronial" in design, though he seems to have simply invented that term. If there is one building that Casa Loma is fashioned after, it would be Balmoral Castle in Scotland, the British royal family's summer residence, where Pellatt visited the future King George V. In truth it is a *mélange* of different styles integrated by Lennox into a building designed to impress the visitor with its imposing size and fortress-like regal air. It

*Lady Mary, Sir Henry, their son Reginald, and his wife Marjorie are served by a maid outside the Hunting Lodge, about 1911.*

is a castle fantasy, drawing on elements of the ancient buildings of Europe, but designed to suit the military imagination of Sir Henry. As one critic put it, Casa Loma is a mixture of seventeenth-century Scottish Baronial and Twentieth Century Fox.

## The Dream Is Built

In December 1909 a building permit was issued to dig the basement, and construction got under way almost immediately. Work stopped for much of 1910 because Sir Henry was busy with his military duties and the trip to Aldershot, but in April 1911 the cornerstone was laid, up to three hundred workers were hired, and construction began in earnest. The work lasted for the next three years.

Despite the appearance of an ancient castle, Casa Loma was built using modern construction techniques. The building is a shell, or box, of reinforced concrete covered with decorative stone. At some points the foundations are forty-five feet deep. The floors are poured concrete, eighteen inches thick. Between each ceiling and the floor above is a four-foot crawl space to allow access to the utilities.

*The Scottish Tower.*

*This photo, taken from the second floor of Casa Loma during construction, shows the gardens and stables.*

The exterior of the building is sheathed in grey sandstone from the Credit River Valley. These stones were cut into long pieces about two inches in depth and mortared onto the concrete by highly skilled stonemasons brought over from Scotland for the job. These stones give a rough, deep-grey appearance. Around each of the windows and doors and along the roof line and terraces is a smooth, lighter grey stone made from an artificial product called Roman stone. This provides an attractive highlight that outlines the features of the castle. The red bronze tile roof, which gleams in the sunshine, gives the house a dramatic look.

All together there were to be ninety-eight rooms in Casa Loma. (Later it came to be called the house of a hundred rooms.) There were many modern conveniences. By the time the Pellatts moved in, Lady Mary suffered from arthritis and diabetes. Since she was often confined to a wheelchair, Sir Henry had an elevator installed for her convenience. Its name is Otis 1, and it is the first elevator in a private home in Canada. There were thirty

bathrooms and twenty-five fireplaces. The electric lighting system was a marvel of its age. Sir Henry had more than five thousand lights installed in Casa Loma, and he could control the entire system from his bedroom. The house also boasted fifty-nine telephones and its own switchboard.

Sir Henry had planned to divert Walmer Road north so that his estate would be unified into one piece of property, but despite his appeals the City of Toronto, which had recently expanded to take in the Casa Loma property, would not allow it. Not to be outdone, Sir Henry built an eight-hundred foot tunnel from the stables to the basement of his castle; this tunnel ran eighteen feet underground so that Pellatt could reach all buildings on the property without going outside.

The basement of the castle was vast. It had twenty-foot ceilings and was to contain an indoor swimming pool, three bowling lanes, a rifle range, and enough room to drill an entire regiment. The wine cellar, with a special cooling system, was one of the greatest on the continent.

No expense was spared. The walls were lined with wooden panelling collected from around the world. In many places the wood was hand carved by master craftsmen. There were gold fixtures in the bathrooms. Plaster ceilings with intricate floral designs were in most of the rooms, small figures were built into prominent nooks, and everywhere the painters and decorators provided colour that highlighted the rooms. Lady Mary's suite, for example, was finished in pale Wedgwood blue and white, her favourite colours.

Once the stonemasons had finished the exterior of the building, they began work on the solid stone wall that was to surround the castle. The wall was six feet wide, ten feet high, and four or more feet deep. It took eighteen months to build and cost $250,000. The stones were hauled from north of Barrie, and Pellatt paid one dollar for each one that was used. When finished, the wall was half a mile in length.

Lennox was involved in every stage of the building of Casa Loma. He checked the levels and used a plumb-line to ensure that the walls were straight. The workmen who were not up to his exacting conditions were soon sent packing. It is said that every one of the stones used in the massive wall was personally inspected by Lennox. Those that did not meet his standards were returned.

Sir Henry also kept close watch over the construction stage and visited almost every day to check on the progress.

Sir Henry lavished money on the furnishings as he did on the construction of the house itself. The Robert Simpson Company, contracted to decorate Casa Loma, engaged a New York interior design company. Europe was scoured for tapestries, silver services, Oriental rugs, Chinese vases, English mantelpieces, and ornate late Victorian and Edwardian furniture. Art work from England and the continent was collected to line the

*Stone masons working on the Casa Loma wall, 1914.*

walls, and Sir Henry bought a number of Canadian pieces that were collector's items. The furnishings alone were estimated to have cost $1.5 million.

But the Pellatts seemed to have almost a cavalier attitude about the cost of Casa Loma. When a group of workmen were installing an expensive, massive chandelier in the dining room, they managed to lose control, and the whole object fell to the floor and shattered. Lady Mary happened to come into the room at precisely this moment. Once she had recovered, she shrugged it off: "Never mind, we'll just order another one."

*The Dining Room.*

Casa Loma and its furnishings were unequalled in North America. It was certainly Toronto's and Canada's most glamorous private home. With its soaring battlements, vast basements, secret passageways, and grand vistas, it was like a page out of a Sir Walter Scott novel, and this effect was precisely what Sir Henry wanted.

The Pellatts had sold their house on Sherbourne Street and another was built for them, just across the street from Casa Loma, where they lived while they were waiting for their new residence to be finished. Finally in the summer of 1914, before Casa Loma was completed, they moved in. But already problems were beginning to gather. In a matter of weeks after they moved into the house, war was declared in Europe. Even more alarming were the rumours that Sir Henry was again having financial difficulties.

*Sir Henry's Study, showing artwork and his replica of Napoleon's desk.*

*The Library, showing the original furnishings.*

*Chapter 6*

# THE DREAM SHATTERS

The year 1910 was the time of Sir Henry Pellatt's greatest triumphs. That was the year of the fiftieth celebrations of the Queen's Own Rifles and the regiment's trip to Aldershot, England, to take part in military manoeuvres. In the same year work began on the basement for Pellatt's dream castle, Casa Loma.

## Speculating on Land

Pellatt had experienced some business set-backs over the years, but generally he did well in the boom years prior to World War I. After 1910 Pellatt shifted his business activities to land speculation. He was convinced that Toronto would soon experience a land boom, and he intended to take advantage of it. He borrowed from a number of banks and financial institutions, using his stocks as collateral, and heavily mortgaged his properties. Casa Loma had a mortgage against it of $1 million.

His method of raising money on property was unusual to say the least. Once he had bought land, he would artificially increase its value by selling it at a much higher price from one company he controlled to another. In 1912, for example, Sir Henry purchased a property between Bathurst Street and Vaughn Road for $316,000. Pellatt paid $116,000 down and took out a mortgage of $200,000. Less than two months later he sold the property to Home City Estates, a company he controlled, for $1,205,000, four times its real value. On the basis of that new value he then borrowed more money and tried to raise money on the company through the stock market. Pellatt was a master at this type of stock transaction, and he had made a great deal of money in this way in the past. However, this time the scheme did not work. The real estate market was depressed, the price of land was going down and few people were building houses. With the debt, and the inflated property valuations, he found it difficult to promote the stocks to higher levels. His entire financial holdings had become very precarious.

One property he did purchase in his own name, in 1912, was a thousand acres of farm land in King Township, twenty miles north of the city. "Lake Marie," he called the property. Sir Henry divided it into four farms, each with their own buildings, stock, and management. There he raised thoroughbred horses, cattle,

*Liberal leader William Lyon Mackenzie King (left), Lady Mary, and Sir Henry (right), 1911. King later became Canada's longest-serving prime minister.*

*Sir Henry and Lady Mary at their Lake Marie property.*

sheep, chickens, guinea fowl, and deer. A rustic stone house was built on the property. Part of its decorations were dozens of stuffed animal trophies, from deer and antelope to pheasants and quail. Once they moved into Casa Loma, the Pellatts began to use the Lake Marie property as a weekend retreat.

By 1912 Sir Henry must have been looking forward to finally slowing down. He was fifty-three years old and beginning to show his age. In that year he retired from his position as commanding officer of the Queen's Own Rifles and became the regiment's honorary colonel. Often he hosted galas and mess dinners, but the everyday responsibility of organizing the regiment now fell to others. Pellatt had spent thirty-six years actively involved with the Queen's Own, eleven of them as the commanding officer. He had left his mark on the regiment and was widely admired by the officers and men for his generosity.

In 1913–14 a short but sharp depression marked the end of the years of economic expansion. With the beginning of World War I, in August 1914, again the economy began to expand and unemployment disappeared. Sir Henry survived this depression, but the value of his holdings was seriously diminished.

Many of his companies were either teetering on the brink of bankruptcy or barely surviving.

## Life in the Castle

In the early summer of 1914 the Pellatts moved into Casa Loma. This should have been a time of celebration of the fulfilment of a dream for Sir Henry and Lady Mary, but money had been slowly drying up, and the castle was not yet finished. Only twenty-three of the ninety-eight rooms were completed. There was scaffolding in the great hall. Sir Henry had heavy curtains put up so the castle's uncompleted state could not be seen by visitors. Many other rooms in the west end, including the billiard room, were unfinished. Window-panes had not yet been installed in many rooms, and windows had to be boarded up to keep out the elements. In the basement the swimming pool, rifle range, and bowling alleys had yet to be finished.

The Pellatts moved into the castle in its unfinished state to cut costs. Sir Henry remained supremely confident when anyone asked about his financial affairs, but he must have been deeply worried. He had mortgaged all of his holdings in the belief that the business climate would get better. The question was, would it improve enough for him to recover his fortune?

Meanwhile the Pellatts were determined to enjoy their

*Sir Henry, in the bow of the canoe, on a hunting expedition with friends.*

new castle even though it was not yet completed. One of Sir Henry's greatest wishes was to be able to host visiting royalty, and although the Prince of Wales, who became the Duke of Windsor after he abdicated the throne, did visit on two occasions, a reigning monarch never came to Casa Loma. Still, there were dinners of a hundred people or more in the beautiful dining room, and often there were social occasions in the conservatory, where the Pellatts loved to show off the flowers and rare plants that they grew in the greenhouses.

In 1912 Lady Mary was asked by Lady Baden-Powell, the wife of the founder of the Boy Scouts, to be the Dominion regent of the Canadian Girl Guides. She was selected in part because of her conservative views. In that era of the suffragette movement, when many women called for voting rights, Lady Mary opposed political change. But she was also selected because she was the wife of Sir Henry, then one of the most prominent, and certainly one of the most generous, businessmen in the country.

Once she was appointed to head the guides, Lady Mary actively promoted the organization by touring the country and visiting the wives of lieutenant governors to gain their help. She also financed various activities of the guides and used Casa Loma as the location for their gatherings. There were demonstrations of first aid by the girls and lavish parties, where tea was poured from silver urns and sipped from delicate, white-and-burnished-gold, china Sheffield cups.

Sir Henry clearly enjoyed his Casa Loma property. Often he would be seen walking in the garden, whistling as he admired the flowers and the grounds. In the war years it

*Lady Mary and Sir Henry review a group of Girl Guides.*

was difficult to get labour, and his money was becoming scarce, but by 1915 much of the castle grounds had been graded and sodded, and shrubs and flowers had been planted. Often in the summer months there were garden parties, and winter activities at Casa Loma included curling, Christmas parties for the servants, and hockey.

The Pellatts had always been generous with charitable organizations, and during the war they devoted even more of their time and money to good causes. They were prominent members of the Anglican Church, and they supported church charities. At one time Sir Henry gave enough money to Trinity College, an Anglican institution within the University of Toronto, to ensure the buildings were repaired and to pay the back salaries of the professors. He gave generously to

*Guests in the Conservatory, 1914.*

*Lady Mary walking in the Casa Loma gardens.*

the Anglican Church and for fifteen years he had been the president of the National Chorus.

Sir Henry was the commissioner of the St. John Ambulance Association for many years and gave generously to that organization. He provided the funds for a complete operating room at Grace Hospital and for schools in the Maritime Provinces. During the war he sent hundreds of packages of food and clothing to members of the Queen's Own Rifles who were prisoners of war in Germany. In the period of World War I, when his assets were shrinking dramatically, Pellatt still tried to continue his charity work. Maybe this was done in part because he enjoyed the attention these gifts gave him and the prestige they gave his business reputation, but it also reflects his great generosity.

## Storm Clouds Gather

As the war ground on, things were getting increasingly difficult. Not only were Sir Henry's business interests taking a beating in the crisis, but his dream castle was becoming a serious liability. The level of property taxes on Casa Loma was an issue he found particularly unfair. The assessment on the property had gone up fivefold, and the taxes were $12,000 a year. He appealed this rate,

arguing that he could never resell Casa Loma and that it was more a liability than an asset, but he lost the appeal. Other costs were also growing. It took forty servants to run the castle, and their salaries totalled $22,000 a year. Heating cost $15,000. It is estimated that it took $100,000 a year just to maintain the grand house.

For the first time in his adult life Pellatt was in serious financial difficulty. Through the war there was inflation, but the value of his property and companies did not inflate at the same rate as other costs. During the war, people put their money into bonds rather than land. The value of property began to decrease, and he found it difficult to meet the payments on his various loans. Pellatt refused to sell land at less than what he considered a fair market price, and so his personal crisis simply got worse.

He was becoming desperate. In November 1915 Pellatt was quoted in the *New York Times* as saying that a company he was involved with would make more than $1 million in profits, a profit level of 50 per cent, on a war contract. Immediately there were accusations from politicians that

*Nineteenth-century French mantel clock in Lady Mary's Suite.*

Pellatt and the company were profiteering. Sir Henry was forced to admit that the claim was not true. As one of his military friends explained, in a weak attempt to try and justify his actions, Pellatt had made this exaggerated report, "for the purpose of booming their stocks." Such an exaggeration was a highly unethical business practice in those days and today would be illegal.

Towards the end of the war Sir Henry developed and promoted La Paz Oil and had it listed on the New York Stock Exchange. With the coming of the automobile age, oil stocks were hot, and he was convinced that this last big deal would be the one that would remake his fortune. But his luck had run out; Pellatt was far too desperate to build a successful company. La Paz drilled in Louisiana but found nothing. Sir Henry began selling his stock for $3.25 when it was listed at $7.00 to $10.00. Soon the company president was attacking Pellatt publicly, and the deal eventually collapsed.

The worst part of this affair was that Sir Henry, in his desperation to make money, sold La Paz shares to servants at Casa Loma. They lost their investment along with all the others who put money into the company. And that was just the beginning of their difficulties. With the collapse of the oil company, Pellatt could not afford to cover the payroll of the servants. For weeks on end, no one was paid. The servants did not want to abandon Sir Henry. He had been a good employer, and there were few jobs during the sharp depression that followed World War I. What were they to do?

By 1923 things were rapidly coming to a conclusion. Pellatt was sixty-four years old, well past the time when he had the confidence, strength of character, and prestige to ride through these difficulties.

*This circa-1854 Heintzman piano is in Lady Mary's Suite.*

## Crisis, Crisis, Crisis

In 1920 the Home Bank was owed close to $2 million by Pellatt and Pellatt, Sir Henry's company. This was one of the three largest loans the bank was carrying, and bank officers knew that they would be vulnerable if the loan were not repaid. They pressured Pellatt to pay up, but he admitted that he did not have the funds and that he owed money to no less than nine financial institutions. It was also clear that most of those institutions did not know the other loans existed. When the Home Bank threatened to sell the securities he had pledged to back the loans, Sir Henry pleaded with them not to do it; he knew the market for the shares would collapse and he would be ruined.

Pellatt played for time, hoping that the fortunes of his companies or the value of his real estate holdings would improve, but they did not. By 1923 the officers of the Home Bank realized that all of Pellatt's affairs were in a mess. One of the officers of the bank wrote: "The possibility of the bank recovering anything from such assets is very greatly outweighed by the embarrassment which would come to it if Pellatt and Pellatt should be forced into bankruptcy."

Time had run out for Sir Henry, and the Home Bank moved in to recover what it could from his dwindling assets. Rather than force him into bankruptcy, the bank compelled him to sign over his entire assets to an investment company. Essentially Pellatt lost control of all of his holdings when he signed that paper. He was finished as a businessman and promoter. For all intents and purposes he was bankrupt.

The year 1923 was a disaster for Sir Henry. Within a month of signing this document he had to vacate Casa Loma, taking a few meagre possessions with him because he could no longer afford to pay the servants, taxes, and upkeep. However, ownership of the property remained in his wife's name. The Pellatts had lived in their dream castle for little more than ten years. The servants did manage to get their back pay, but they lost their jobs. Less than a month after the Home Bank forced Pellatt to restructure his affairs, the bank was itself bankrupt. One of the chief causes of this bankruptcy was Sir Henry Pellatt's default on his loans. Through this crisis Lady Pellatt's health had been deteriorating, and finally, within a year after the Pellatts left Casa Loma, on April 15, 1924, Lady Mary died.

But luck was still with Sir Henry on two accounts: because he had managed to sign the agreement with the bank before it collapsed, he was absolved of all liability for the mess that he had created, and because he avoided personal bankruptcy by turning his assets over to the investment company, he was able to retain his knighthood.

## The Auction of the Century

The period from 1914 to 1923 had been disastrous for Sir Henry. He had seen his fabulous fortune evaporate; he had lacked the funds to finish his magnificent house; his prestige in the business community had been shattered; he had been forced to abandon his dream house; and he was living in an apartment when his wife died. But there was one final trial he had to face. Between June 23 and 27, 1924, the entire movable contents of the castle were sold to the highest bidder at what was called the "auction of the century."

People from as far away as Montreal, Detroit, and New York came to pick through the leavings of Sir Henry and find a bargain, but most

were members of Toronto's social and business élite. From the time the first bid was registered until the last sale was made, people packed into the castle.

There was a kind of excited carnival atmosphere as the bargains came thick and fast. A solid silver tea caddy went for $18. A Chippendale lacquer cabinet with engraved brass mounts went for $410. Two grizzly bearskins with head and claws went for $35 and $46. An invalid's wheelchair (presumably used by Lady Mary) sold for $6. Sir Henry's own bed, a Louis XVI bedstead in mahogany, richly embellished with gilt, with box spring and hair mattress, went for $380.

Sir Henry's fabulous art collection, worth a great deal of money, was sold for a song. A Homer Watson painting went for $55. A Rembrandt sold for $25, a William Hogarth for $60, and a W. Armstrong for $17.50. Some of the art work got respectable prices. A John Constable painting sold for $875, a Turner for $5,100, a Sir Joshua Reynolds for $2,700, a Kreighoff for $120, and five paintings by Charles M. Russell went for a total of $1,550, but all of these paintings were much more valuable. Today, if it could be established that they were originals, they could fetch up to $1 million each. The magnificent collection that cost $1.5 million and took years to assemble was gone, and the total proceeds of the auction, which went to the creditors, were a mere $131,600.

*Fancy Victorian barometer located in the Conservatory.*

On the fourth and final day of the auction a reporter found Sir Henry wandering through the castle and asked him to comment on his feelings about the sale. "The process was something like having a tooth pulled," he explained. "Once over, one proceeded to forget all about it." The experience must have been difficult for someone as proud as Sir Henry. The auction sale dramatically underlined that the fabulous Pellatt fortune had all but disappeared.

## The Fading Years

After leaving the castle, the Pellatts lived in the city for a time, and then, when his wife died, Sir Henry moved out to his Lake Marie farm, north of Toronto. There he lived quietly. He was finished with business, but he puttered around the farm, taking an interest in the animals and the local social calendar.

*Sir Henry with his second wife, the former Catharine Welland Merritt, shortly after their marriage, 1927.*

It was there that he was honoured by the Queen's Own Rifles for fifty years of service to the regiment. During the war Sir Henry had been promoted to brigadier general, and in 1921 he was given the rank of major general. These were honorary titles, but they reflected that the military still held him in esteem. On June 28, 1926, a party was held at Lake Marie to honour all he had done for his regiment.

It was a lovely, warm summer day. The farm was beautifully decorated with an archway and flowers for the event. The old soldier was dressed immaculately in his blue-and-gold brigadier general's uniform topped with the scarlet-and-white feathers of his plumed hat. Sir Henry received the many guests out on the lawn. Then he took the salute as the Queen's Own regimental band marched by with five hundred officers and men under the command of his son, Colonel Reginald Pellatt, who was now the commanding officer of the unit. As a final tribute three biplanes from Camp Borden flew past, and the National Chorus, which Sir Henry had supported financially for many

years, sang a tribute. A gold-handled ceremonial sword was given to him by the regiment in appreciation of his years of service.

The next year Sir Henry seemed to be ready to start life again. In March 1927 he married Catharine Welland Merritt, an old family friend, in St. Catharines. She came from a Loyalist family, and her grandfather had built the first Welland Canal. The groom was sixty-eight and the bride was sixty-one. The wedding was a rather modest affair, compared with other events in Sir Henry's life. Afterwards the couple moved out to the farm in King Township. Unfortunately, a little over a year and a half later, the new Mrs. Pellatt became sick and died of cancer. Once again Sir Henry was alone.

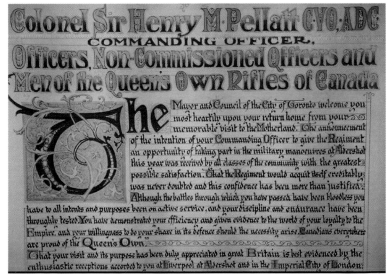

*Sir Henry received many commemorative certificates honouring his years of service to the Queen's Own Rifles.*

## Chapter 7
# THE CASTLE FINDS A NEW LIFE

After Sir Henry left Casa Loma, the grand house was badly neglected. For two winters it sat vacant. Those who attended the auction after the first winter with no heat in the castle noticed broken windows and damage to some of the plaster. At the end of the second winter with no heat, the damage was even greater. There was concern that, if it was not occupied, there could be permanent damage to the structure.

*From 1925 to 1929, groups tried to establish an apartment hotel at Casa Loma.*

### The Apartment-Hotel Era

Casa Loma was owned by the estate of Lady Mary Pellatt and managed by Sir Henry. In 1925 he arranged a long-term lease to W.F. Sparling, an architect who wanted to develop it as an apartment-hotel and a show-place for parties and entertainment.

When Sparling took over the castle, he found it in bad shape, and he began the process of repairing the damage and finishing some of the rooms. The great hall and the billiard room were completed during this time. Sparling also took down the wall between the library and the dining room, replacing it with pillars. This enlarged space became a dance floor, and Casa Loma for a time was a favourite night spot.

A musician by the name of Glen Gray played at the castle with a band called the Orange Blossoms in 1927. In 1933 the band was renamed Glen Gray and the Casa Loma Orchestra. It became one of North America's most famous groups in the big band era.

W.F. Sparling had only modest success with his apartment-hotel, but he planned a $1 million expansion of the complex. He designed two massive wings, one to the east and another to the west of the building, each with ninety-six suites and fifty-six rooms. However, he had difficulty financing the project. A New York group offered to buy it in 1928, but the deal was never consummated. Finally the hotel failed in 1929 with the onset of the Depression.

Once again Casa Loma returned to Sir Henry Pellatt. He listed it for sale for $700,000, but no one was interested. Now it was clear that it was a colossal white elephant that no one could afford to own or keep up. The Depression seemed to seal the fate of the great house; the stock market crash wiped out what little reserves Sir Henry had left. He did not even have enough money to help his son, who had lost everything, including the old company of Pellatt and Pellatt. Casa Loma sat vacant, and none of the bills were paid. Finally in 1933 the city took the property for $27,305.45 in back taxes.

### Kiwanis Saves the Day

What to do with such a huge private house? No one, particularly during the Depression, could afford to live in a place that large. There were suggestions at city council that it should be torn down, but many felt that would be destroying a significant part of the city's heritage. Mary Pickford made enquiries about using it for a movie stu-

*Casa Loma was first opened to visitors by the Kiwanis Club in 1937.*

dio, but nothing came of them. Other suggestions included using it as a high school, art gallery, museum, local firehall, a war veterans convalescence home, an Orange lodge, a millionaires club, a home for the royal family, a railway stop, and later a permanent residence for the Dionne quintuplets.

Meanwhile the castle sat empty. Every winter the frost did more damage. Windows were broken by local children. The once wonderful gardens became overgrown with weeds. Trees and shrubs grew wild. The longer it stood vacant, the more it seemed that demolition was inevitable.

But there always was interest in Casa Loma. Maybe it was the size, the location, the beauty of the building, or interest in Sir Henry Pellatt. Whatever it was, people often came to look at the castle. Then Bill Bothwell, of the West Toronto Kiwanis Club, made the suggestion that his organization run Casa Loma as a tourist attraction, and in 1936 the city agreed to try out the idea.

When the Kiwanis Club took over, the building was in terrible shape. This is how Bothwell later described it:

The castle was indescribable ... There were over 2,500 panes of diamond plate glass broken. The place was all boarded up, but on the Davenport Road side boys or someone had broken through and there were birds by the hundreds in the main rotunda which was filled with nests and filth ... We took out two dump truck loads of filth off the floor.

It was the Kiwanis Club that saved Casa Loma and preserved it for future generations. They worked hard to restore it, and in 1937 it was opened as a tourist attraction at twenty-five cents per visitor.

In August of that year Sir Henry was invited to a banquet to address the Kiwanis Club. To cover his debts he had sold his Lake Marie farm in 1935 to the Catholic Church to be used as a retreat, and now lived in an apartment in the city. He had lost almost seventy pounds, looked frail and gaunt, and used a cane to steady himself. Cataracts had made him almost blind. But although his shirt and suit

*Sir Henry signs the Casa Loma guest book on a visit hosted by the Kiwanis in 1937.*

were out of fashion and did not fit him any more, they were immaculately pressed. To everyone he was gracious and courtly in his manners.

As he rose to speak the Kiwanis members and their wives stood to sing "Old Soldiers Never Die." Sir Henry covered his face with his hands to hide his tears. When he regained his composure he repeated the first line of the song: "Old soldiers never die, they just fade away." After a moment he was able to continue:

I assure you I have my feelings, and I cannot help them. I am delighted to be here, and I am sorry it has affected me so. I built Casa Loma principally as a place where people would enjoy themselves. Your club is now using it for that purpose and bringing enjoyment and happiness to countless people. It could not be put to better use. I am satisfied.

*The old soldier considers a painting of himself in earlier days.*

tered instrument cases and hauled out brass horns of various shapes and sizes. This was all that was left of the 1910 polished military brass band of the Queen's Own Rifles. The musicians assembled in the hall and entered the packed ballroom playing the regimental march. In they came, heads erect, marching briskly, valiantly playing their tarnished horns that most had not touched in years. Every man in the room came to his feet shouting, cheering, and waving napkins in the air. After a march around the room, someone started to sing a song that had been sung by members of the regiment for decades:

*The Queen's Own Rifles, they came this way,*
*And broke things up in an awful way.*
*You can bet your life there'll be hell to pay*
*When the Queen's Own Rifles come back this way.*

On his eightieth birthday, January 6, 1939, Sir Henry was honoured at a banquet at the Royal York by 225 men from the Queen's Own Rifles whom he had taken with him to Aldershot, England in 1910, so many years before. It was an evening of tribute to Sir Henry, nostalgic reminiscences and the good cheer of old comrades at arms. The theme song of the evening was "Has Anyone Here Seen Henry?" sung to the tune of "Has Anyone Here Seen Kelly?"

After the dinner a scant dozen men fished into bat-

At the centre of it all, standing at the head table, gazing across the scene stood Major-General Sir Henry Pellatt. Those close to him said that there was a mistiness in his eye.

The climax of the evening for the royalists among them came with the reading of a telegram to Sir Henry from none other than Queen Mary herself. "Your Colonel-in-Chief has great pleasure in sending you warmest congratulations on the occasion of your eightieth birthday."

Afterwards Sir Henry was invited to speak. He struggled to his feet. He had not been well, and many in the room remarked on the feebleness of their once-robust commanding officer. Tears were coursing down his cheeks. "I'm delighted to see so many of the boys of the old brigade here. Old boys did I say?" And then with a smile, "Why, dammit, you look like a fine bunch of men to me right now."

## The Funeral March

Two months later Sir Henry was dead. He had lived the last year of his life with his chauffeur, Tom Ridgway, in

*Sir Henry's casket is carried out of St. James Cathedral.*

a small, nondescript house in the Toronto suburb of Rexdale. He died penniless, with debts of more than $6,000 and only $185 in cash. Born in rags, he had risen to riches beyond the imagination of most people, and then his fortune collapsed, forcing him to live in poverty again. His life had a fairy-tale quality much like the dream castle that he built.

In death the reputation of Sir Henry seemed to recover its former stature. The Queen's Own Rifles honoured him with a full military funeral. A collection was made among the men, and $650 was raised to pay the costs. For three days the body lay in Reginald Pellatt's home at 328 Walmer Road, across the street from Casa Loma; the only wreath by Sir Henry's casket was the one from the men of the Queen's Own Rifles.

The funeral service was held on a cold March Saturday afternoon, in St. James Cathedral on King Street East. Thousands of people filled the cavernous church. There were flowers in profusion. Through the ceremony, members of the Queen's Own stood guard, heads bowed, hands on their rifles. After the service the trumpet played the

"Last Post" and then "Reveille."

The casket was carried outside and placed on a gun carriage. Three hundred and fifty members of the Queen's Own Rifles, dressed in heavy greatcoats, formed up around the carriage, and the procession began the slow march down King Street, past the building where Pellatt and Pellatt had its offices, past the site of the Home Bank, the Albany Club, and all the other places of business that Sir Henry had known so well. On the casket was his cocked brigadier general's hat with the white-and-scarlet feathers blowing in the cold wind. Behind the gun carriage came a riderless horse with reversed boots in the stirrups. Then came the regimental sergeant major carrying a purple cushion with Sir Henry's ten military decorations.

At Richmond Street the body was placed in a hearse and taken to the Forest Lawn Mausoleum. There, volley after

*His casket is borne through the streets on a gun carriage.*

volley was fired into the air by a squad of twelve riflemen until the only smell was that of gunpowder and cordite. Again the bugles sounded the "Last Post" and "Reveille," and the military party was dismissed to leave family and friends as his remains were placed beside his wife Mary.

People from all walks of life had lined the streets to watch the funeral procession of a man who had been so much a part of the life of their city. It was the largest funeral ever held in Toronto. On that day, at the very end of the depression and on the brink of another world war, Sir Henry must have been remembered as a man from another era when the financial capitalist held sway over the lives of thousands, when there was a belief in the importance of the British Empire, and when the pomp and ceremony of the military were central elements of Canadian life.

Some may have come to the funeral to honour those things, but most came because Sir Henry had been a character who lived life in a grand style and was generous

*The regimental Sergeant Major carried Sir Henry's medals on a purple pillow.*

to a fault. As one of his friends said: "He gave pleasure. He made and left his mark and had a grand time."

*Following military tradition, a riderless horse, with reversed boots in the stirrups, marks the fallen soldier.*

# AFTERWORD

Since Pellatt's day Casa Loma has blossomed into one of the great attractions of the city. The Kiwanis Club has done more than restore it to its former greatness. Rooms that had never been completed have been finished, and a program of redecoration has brought back the richness of some of the rooms.

The objective of the program is to restore and refurbish the castle to match the first conception of E.J. Lennox and Sir Henry. This is a slow process, but much has been accomplished. The greatest difficulty has been to replace the furniture and art work that were auctioned off in 1924; however, some of the furnishings have been returned to the castle. A number of families in Toronto own pieces that were originally from Casa Loma. Lifestyles change, and many find that they do not have room for these objects any longer. Over the years there has been a steady stream of furniture back to the castle.

*The castle exterior and gardens today.*

The same, unfortunately, cannot be said for Sir Henry's art collection. Some of those pieces have found their way into art galleries around North America, while others remain highly prized possessions in private homes.

The castle has been used primarily as a tourist attraction since it was leased to the Kiwanis Club in 1936, but this has not been its only use. During World War II the stables were the location of a top secret military project. ASDIC was a new electronic device invented by the British to detect submarines. The production centre in England was destroyed by bombs, and the British Admiralty came to Canada, looking for a place to carry on the assembly of the devices.

William Corman, a Toronto engineer, was asked to head the project. Corman looked for a safe place where the devices could be assembled without any suspicion. Secretly he approached the Kiwanis Club president, and Bothwell agreed to set up an assembly factory in the stables. Through the latter part of the war, dairy, bread, and flower trucks would arrive with machine parts. Quietly twenty people worked in the stables, assembling these parts into ASDIC devices. As Corman later said: "No saboteur worth his salt would bother with a freak castle crawling with pleasure seekers."

Since the war, there have been other uses for the castle. In the 1940s and 1950s it was a favourite dance spot where many famous bands played. Wedding parties often use the large rooms and gardens for receptions, and associations, business groups, and individuals frequently hold functions in the castle.

A recent use of Casa Loma has been as a movie and television location site. More than one horror film has been shot in the cavernous basement, and movies requiring gracious nineteenth- or early twentieth-century settings have often been filmed in the gardens, terraces, and elegant formal rooms of the castle.

The maintenance of Casa Loma is a shared responsibility. The Kiwanis Club maintains the interior of the building while the City of Toronto, the actual owner of the castle, takes responsibility for the outside maintenance. Pellatt built the structure with the best of materials, but there has been some deterioration. An extensive program of restoration is ongoing.

In one of the important recent developments, in 1987 the Garden Club of Toronto took on the task of renovating the gardens of Casa Loma. Sir Henry and Lady Pellatt loved their gardens, and the Garden Club has successfully recaptured the romantic spirit of the castle's grounds. Today the gardens are maintained by the Casa Loma gardening staff and are open to the public.

One of Sir Henry's dreams was that after his death Casa Loma would become a military museum. Today much of the third floor of the castle honours his old regiment, the Queen's Own Rifles, one of the most famous army units in Canada. His dream has been realized, not in the way he originally conceived it, but in a way that would please the old soldier.

The Kiwanis Club runs the castle as a non-profit venture, putting some of the funds it raises back into the maintenance and restoration of the building. The rest it uses to support many other organizations and a wide variety of charitable events. In the last ten years alone the Kiwanis Club of Casa Loma has contributed more than $2.6 million to numerous charitable projects out of their revenues from the castle.

In some ways Sir Henry is a tragic figure. He worked all of his life to make money to build his dream castle, but in the end he lost it all: his money, his castle, and his social position. And yet Pellatt is anything but a tragic figure. In Casa Loma he has left Torontonians a legacy of an earlier age when dreams of castles could become a reality. The building is big, optimistic, and confident, like the man himself. It is an expression of an era when a financier, with dreams of an empire, could make his mark on the country. Casa Loma is Sir Henry Pellatt's gift to us all, and he would be happy to see the throngs of people who continue to enjoy it.

## Sources

A book such as this could never have been written without building on the work of earlier researchers. I am particularly indebted to Carlie Oreskovich's excellent biography on Sir Henry Pellatt. Anyone wanting a more detailed description of Pellatt's many activities should consult this book.

Over the years the Casa Loma staff has collected material on the Pellatts, the castle and its original furnishings and art work. This material is available at Casa Loma at a modest cost.

The career of Sir Henry was closely followed by journalists working for the daily press. The insights of these journalists give a freshness and immediacy to events that is hard to capture decades later. This material is sometimes difficult to find but usually worth the effort. The best place to look is in the Metropolitan Toronto Reference Library.

The following list of books includes those that have been published on Pellatt and Casa Loma as well as a short list of standard works on Canadian business history.

**Casa Loma and Sir Henry Pellatt**

Denison, John. Casa Loma and the Man who Built It. Toronto: Boston Mills Press, 1982.

Flint, David. Henry Pellatt. Toronto: Fitzhenry & Whiteside Limited, 1979.

Oreskovich, Carlie. Sir Henry Pellatt: The King of Casa Loma. Toronto: Casa Loma, 1996.

**Canadian Business History**

Bliss, Michael. Northern Enterprise: Five Centuries of Canadian Business. Toronto: McClelland and Stewart, 1987.

Naylor, Tom. The History of Canadian Business (Vol. 1 and 2). Toronto: James Lorimer and Company, Publishers, 1975.

Taylor, Graham D., and Peter A. Baskerville. A Concise History of Business in Canada. Toronto: Oxford University Press, 1994.